75 Years of Christian Witness

A HISTORY
OF THE LENAH VALLEY BAPTIST
CHURCH, HOBART, TASMANIA

by
Laurence F. Rowston and
Maurice French

CONTENTS

Foreword 5

Preface 7

Beginnings 9

Establishing a Church Fellowship in Lenah Valley 14

Building Our Spiritual Home 19

Passing the Baton 30

The Bohm Boom 39

An On-going Time of Ministry 46

One Church Two Locations 52

Stretching Our Tent Pegs – Welcoming the Nepalese 57

75 Years and Counting 66

Appendices – Various Pastors' Histories 74

Lenah Valley Baptist Church Timeline 81

FOREWORD

It is a delight to write this foreword to another book by Laurie Rowston focussing in on parts of the history of Tasmanian Baptists.

I first came across Laurie's work when I began as interim pastor at Hobart Baptist Church in 2010. Within weeks, I was handed a copy of *One Hundred Years of Witness* (1984) which outlined the history of "The Tab" as it is affectionately known. It proved to be an extremely valuable resource.

Having arrived in Tasmania early in 1981, Laurie soon became co-editor of the *Hobart Baptist Church News* before taking on co-editorship of the *Tasmanian Baptist Advance* in mid-1984. After twenty-eight years as editor and about 130 issues later, Laurie announced his retirement in September 2013.

In the years since, Laurie has spent many hours scouring historical records, collating myriads of pieces of information and producing many and various histories pertaining to Tasmanian Baptists, its churches and its pastors. Since becoming Mission Director of Tasmanian Baptists, Laurie's history on the early years of the Baptist Union of Tasmania titled, *Spurgeon's Men* (2011) has been very helpful in understanding our roots.

The book you are now holding, *75 Years of Witness: A History of the Lenah Valley Baptist Church, Hobart* [2023] is another example of Laurie's fine work. As you read it, you will experience his unique skill of pulling together information from various sources and taking you on a brief and brisk, yet thorough walk-through history. Along the way he draws your attention to important facts and significant events without judgement.

Like any church, *Lenah Valley Baptist Church* is not really about the building or its organisational structure, but about the people, the relationships and the fellowship they enjoy. Here again, we are indebted to Laurie who keeps the focus where it should be, on the people - their contributions, growth and legacy.

I'm sure you will find it encouraging. So many lives have been touched, enriched and changed over the past seventy-five years. And it is all because of the hard work of the named and unnamed people who loved, worked, forgave and prayed together. It is they who are the history of Lenah Valley Baptist Church. They did it all for the love and glory of God. May they inspire us to do the same.

Stephen Baxter, March 2023
Mission Director for Tasmanian Baptists

Cover Art by Isaac Rai (2023) based on original architechtural drawings by Hartley Wilson and Bolt 1959.

Isaac Rai arrived in Australia in 2011 as a refuge from Nepal and now calls Australia home. An accomplished artist, Isaac shares of his humble beginnings:

"Conditions in the refugee camp were very basic. In 1994 I learnt to draw and paint but we didn't have enough money for materials so we used natural colour pigments from plants and flowers. We made our brushes by feathering' the end of worn out felt tip pens and painted on blank pages from exercise books. My art reflects my journey. I once was trapped in a refugee camp without money or freedom. Now I am free to roam, with the security of a house and a job."

Isaac is a committed member of the Hobart Nepalese Church, one of the Citywide Baptist Church congregations since 2011.

PREFACE

This year, 2023, sees the 75th anniversary of the commencement of a Sunday school in Lenah Valley which was at the time a fast-growing housing area for middle class families. This short history gives an account of what has taken place since 1948. The school began in a time of what could be described as a high point in Christian enterprise in Australia, during the post War years when Sunday Schools were bursting with children and where the local church was still a family community centre. The other such time was the 1870s and 1880s, the heyday for non-conformists, when all that one needed to do to gain a congregation was to erect a chapel; people were expected to come.

As the author of the text, it would be the height of ingratitude to release this book without an expression of thanks to one of the church's long-term members, Maurice French. Over many years Maurice has collected the church's annual reports, notices, bulletins and more and put them in chronological order in arch-folders and I was able to utilise this amazing collection for what follows. What he had collected would not have been available to me without extended and demanding research by me over many months. His compilation also indicated areas still needing some work. Maurice also attended to the placement of the many photographs. I used "Trove" to discover fascinating details of the lives of some of the pastors and especially that of the Rev. John Toroni.

The impact of various pastors on the life of the church varied and the accounts of their pastorates give serious hints to what succeeds and what does not even in our day. I confess that I have written their biographies in such a way that the majority have "received prizes" and so they should.

It must be admitted that this book purposely fails to make an extended reference to a number of the faithful who attended and supported the work financially as well as showing tenacious loyalty. Without them there would be no church. Some of these were core members who oversaw the work for decades and whose commitment could not be questioned. To these unnamed workers the church owes a great debt. This history would be far larger in size if every one of these persons was mentioned.

I am indebted to a number of others who made this history possible. One is Maurice French's wife Christine who was present from the commencement of the Sunday school. There are others who have proof read the work and made valuable suggestions. The final format was made possible through the expertise of Dan Evenhuis, Executive Pastor of the Citywide Baptist Church.

The greatest care has been taken to ensure accuracy in the various matters dealt with. If there are any mistakes, they are not mistakes of carelessness. It is our wish that those readers who have lived through these years will experience enriching memories. This book is not just a collection of stories, but a family story of those who were brought together in the bundle of life.

We look back on these earlier days not in order that we might live in the past, rather that its challenges will spur us on to greater things. This knowledge of our beginnings saves us from overvaluing the new or glorifying the past. Through an understanding of these events we can move on with confidence and continue to fulfill our role of being the salt of the earth and being a light unto the world. But the challenge of the future is also the challenge of the present; tomorrow grows out of today. We live in pressing times as faith has suffered an eclipse in that the habit of church attendance has ebbed, there is less appeal to the Good News of Jesus and the Sunday school, the driving force of this church at the beginning, is no more.

Even so we trust that this book will prove attractive and readable to Baptists and non-Baptists alike.

Laurence Rowston (MA)
Historian for the Baptist Churches of Tasmania

BEGINNINGS

The work began when the Hobart Baptist Tabernacle under the leadership of the Rev. Edward Roberts-Thomson saw a need for outreach in the growing suburb of Lenah Valley. To that end an afternoon Sunday school was commenced in the Community Hall on 1 August 1948. The staffing and the work were carried out under the superintendence of Les Reardon, a lay-preacher from the Tabernacle.

Christine French who was there in the beginning, remembers those early days,
> My older brother and sister took me as a four year old along to the Community Hall where I remember holding the hymn book and pretending to read the songs. We didn't go every Sunday afternoon; sometimes we'd catch the tram and go into the Hobart Tabernacle where I remember sitting in a circle in the upstairs Kindy room.
> Sunday school was a time for girls to wear their prettiest dresses, hats and even little lacy gloves. Its anniversaries were the times when we wore our new dresses, mine made by Mum. Numbers were high and at some anniversaries, held in the old RSL Hall, now the Guides Hall, we could reach the ceiling as we stood on the raised stands. At the time there were yearly Sunday school exams which included memorizing verses of the Bible.

The district was growing quite rapidly following the end of World War II and this afternoon Sunday school was the only Christian witness in the suburb at that time. Like so many other Baptist churches in the State, this church grew from a children's work. The annual Sunday school picnics were grand affairs with many held at Taroona. Sometimes the school would catch the ferry "Cartela" to South Arm; another time it involved a train journey to the Mount Field National Park.

On 24 February 1952 evening services commenced in the suburb's R.S.L. Hall. They were originally intended to be held fortnightly, but there was sufficient interest shown to carry on at weekly intervals. To assist, the Baptist Home Mission provided a monthly financial subsidy.

Rev S. J. M. Holly
Minister Hobart Baptist Church, 1950-1962

The Hobart Baptist Church, now under the leadership of the Rev. Merlyn Holly, wanted the Tabernacle to continue oversight of the development of the school, but the four Lenah Valley families of Frank Kelly, Andrew Lawry, BAF Wolnizer and David Oxley still working with Les Reardon, wanted to develop the work on their own and bring into existence a Baptist Church. On 9 November 1952 the Hobart Church agreed and Les Reardon resigned as the Sunday school Superintendent as he was not a resident in the district. The Fellowship now operated independently and Andrew Lawry was appointed school Superintendent.

Andrew Lawry

Andrew Lawry grew up in Ivanhoe, Victoria, and when he came to Tasmania he was employed as the Chief Accountant for The Mercury newspaper. He later became its Chief Executive Officer. He is remembered as a very charming, friendly, compassionate and caring man and served the Lenah Valley church very faithfully for many years.

Andrew Lawry remained School Superintendent for many years and at one stage every child living in Brushy Creek

Road, the street in which the Lawry family lived, was a scholar in the school. The grand children of Roy Cazaly, of "Up There Cazaly", the football anthem of the AFL, also lived in this street and they too attended. The staff of the Sunday school were expected to attended its teachers' meetings and undertake home visitation of children's families.

Dr Frank Kelly – Dec 1959

For a time some children in the School were invited to Sunday dinner at the Lawry's home and among them was Christine French (nee Filby). "This felt extra special," she remembers, "as we joined the family sitting down to a yummy roast dinner. Muriel would rush home between the end of Sunday School and the beginning of church to prepare the meal, something which many of the congregation have since also done."

Christine continues, "Andrew Lawry had an amazing gift of keeping up with each child and church member: what was happening in their lives, how their school and studies were progressing, any family events and changes, and would produce cuttings from his prolific newspaper files which would be relevant or helpful to each person."

Lenah Valley Baptist Kinders - 1952

On one occasion he appealed to the Hobart Baptist Church for additional teachers and so in response on one Sunday, when his eldest son Russell, Len Harvey and Maurice French were standing outside the church talking, the Rev Merlyn Holly pointed to them saying, "You are needed next Sunday at Lenah Valley and you are to report to Mr Lawry!" They duly turned up at the Lenah Valley Community Hall the following Sunday afternoon.

Len Harvey later trained at the WEC College in St Leonards before taking up missionary service in The Gambia in West Africa.

It was through the Sunday school work that Maurice met his future wife, Christine. Some Sundays, he would pick her up with friend Beth Kelly in a vintage hearse which was an interesting way to be driven to Sunday School!

Lenah Valley Baptist Sunday School - 1952

It was on 7 February 1952 in the RSL hall in Lenah Valley Road that the morning services commenced. On many occasions on the Saturday evenings for those who had the task of setting up for the Sunday morning services, it meant patiently waiting outside until the last stragglers of the previous nights "do" had left. Then it was time to open the doors and bring out the mops and brooms to rid the floor of drink slops and clear the air of the pervading smell of alcohol!

RSL Hall, Lenah Valley - 1960

ESTABLISHING A CHURCH FELLOWSHIP IN LENAH VALLEY

The Rev. John Toroni

By late 1952 the fellowship committed itself to a musical-gospel mission conducted by the American violinist-evangelist from Philadelphia, the Rev. John Toroni. He was accompanied by his wife Eunice. The mission was to take place the following January and February.

Rev John & Eunice Toroni with Joan

This was their first public mission in Tasmania and they commenced in the Lenah Valley R.S.L. hall. Following the mission, the fellowship invited him to pastor the Fellowship for a period of six months, which he accepted, but only after they had conducted another tour in NSW and SA. The Hobart Mission commenced in May 1953 and concluded at the end of October. Advertising was extensive for their special events at both the Lenah Valley RSL and Lenah Valley Community halls. They then embarked on a twelve month mission across Tasmania.

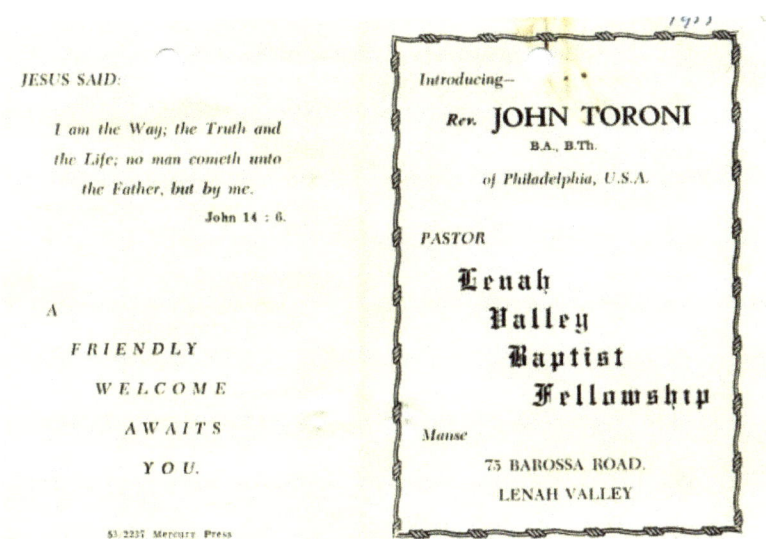

At this stage the Baptist Home Mission was not involved in the Lenah Valley work, having its hands full with the viability of the South Hobart Church. On 4 November 1953 a request was submitted to the Baptist Union over the signatures of Dr Frank Kelly and his wife Enid, Mr Andrew Lawry and his wife Muriel and Mrs Marie Paice, Muriel's mother, for the request that the Lenah Valley work now be constituted as a Home Mission Fellowship. These five had initially sought to have Lenah Valley Fellowship constituted as a church, but this was not possible as the Act of Incorporation of the Baptist Union of Tasmania, passed by the Parliament of Tasmania years earlier, required a minimum of five male members over the age of twenty-one and there were not yet five males. So the Baptist Union constituted the work as a Home Mission Fellowship.

The Rev Trevor Fist

While there was little response from the non-Christian families whose children were attending the Sunday school to join in the work, the school itself flourished. The numbers increased particularly in the kindergarten and primary age groups, but not so in the Intermediates. A Bible Class had yet to form but this was understandable as the district was generally made up of young families.

The Home Mission then initiated a South Hobart-Lenah Valley pastorate. Although South Hobart Church began in 1943, Rev Trevor Fist's appointment was its first sustained ministry. To begin with Mr Fist preached at South Hobart for all the evening services and at just one morning service with the remainder of the morning services preached at Lenah Valley. This arrangement of a joint pastorate was contingent upon suitable accommodation being obtained. Financially neither South Hobart nor Lenah Valley could provide this, so a temporary arrangement was made which resulted in the Fists having the use of a portion of a house at 159 Augusta Road in Lenah Valley. But the owner soon put the house on the market, so rapid negotiations took place to obtain finance to purchase it at his figure of £2,520. Once the sale went through, renovations followed. At its official opening the Legion of Donors donated £32. Still the Home Mission could not assist financially due to restraints.

It had been agreed that Trevor Fist should only be employed in the joint pastorate for three years and this was held to and he departed at the end of March 1957 for a pastorate at the Deloraine

Baptist Church. During this joint pastorate in Hobart, two senior Sunday school scholars and two of the scholars' parents were baptised. The Sunday school continued to grow and in 1955 a youth group was formed. "Special" Sunday school events included a three week Daily Vacation Bible School in April 1955 conducted by the Rev. S. A. McDonald, who was at the time the Superintendent of the Sydney City Mission. While there was a good team of helpers for the Vacation School, there were no conspicuous results. However, Rev McDonald's short ministry to the adults was a great blessing. On the 18th March 1955 we held our first meeting of the Baptist Youth Fellowship in the R.S.L. Hall under the leadership of Mrs Lawry.

A White and Warn Mission took place in October 1955 with an overall attendance of 280 children over the five days. These two men, Jack White and Milton Warn, were "The Modern Pied Pipers" of the Victorian Baptist Christian Education Council. Christine French retains a vivid memory of the Primary school children eagerly streaming across the John Turnbull Park to the RSL Hall when the Primary school concluded for the day. The children were eager to participate in what White and

6th ANNIVERSARY

10th   11th

October 1954

LENAH VALLEY BAPTIST
SUNDAY SCHOOL

Sunday, 10th October — R.S.L. HALL
   11 a.m. REV. TREVOR FIST
   2.45 p.m. MR. IAN BOSS-WALKER
(Prizes for Cradle Roll, Kindergarten & Primary will be awarded during afternoon)

Monday, 11th October — R.S.L. HALL
   7.30 p.m. CHILDREN'S CONCERT AND SENIOR PRIZE AWARDS

YOU ARE CORDIALLY INVITED

DON'T just send your children - - - -
                              BRING them.

Warn had in store. Such was the overflow on the final evening that the front doors of the hall had to be removed so those on the porch could get a viewing.

These two missionaries from Victoria were at the time also visiting other Tasmanian Baptist Churches. Their missions were much appreciated as they assisted both churches and Sunday schools.

By mid 1956 sixty families were regularly sending their children to the Sunday school. 50% of the older Baptist Churches across the State were at the time not experiencing such good turnouts. This meant that over 200 adults and children were being contacted through the work. The first baptisms took place at the Hobart Baptist Tabernacle in 1956 with the candidates being Wanda King (nee Tapp) and Graeme Kelly.

J B White & M Warn – Mission LVBC 1955

BUILDING OUR SPIRITUAL HOME

The current church site at 2 Pottery Road was purchased in 1956. The block of land had been available in 1952 for a price of about £600, but due to lack of denominational support, it was not possible to purchase it at the time. It came back on the market in 1956 with a price tag of £950. The purchase was agreed to as there was no other worthwhile site remaining in the suburb which was suitable for a Church building. The Augusta Road tram line from Hobart terminated at the Pottery Road crossing and this was but a short step to the church site. Finance to purchase the site was obtained by private arrangements as gifts, from Church funds and a loan of £200 from the Home Mission. By the time two thirds of the purchase price had been paid off, the Home Mission liquidated the balance.

The Rev Tom A. L. Green

In 1958 a four-way cooperative arrangement, designated the Southern Regional Pastoral Committee, was formed between the Home Mission Committee, the Hobart and the South Hobart Churches and Lenah Valley Fellowship. The Rev. Thomas A. L. Green, associate pastor of the Hobart Church, was given the responsibility for the

Rev & Mrs Green - 1961

Laying the Foundation Stone – 17 July 1960

work at Lenah Valley and South Hobart. His previous pastorate of six years had been at the Wynyard Baptist Church. His ministry in Hobart proved difficult because of the divided responsibilities especially during the initial period when he was expected to also assist with youth work in the Hobart Church. After an initial period, he was freed from this added responsibility. By 17 June 1959 the morning services at South Hobart ceased, due to poor attendances, although the evening services continued.

On 17 July 1960, with a building fund of nearly £1,000 in hand, the foundation stone was laid for the church building. The architect was Dirk Bolt of Architects, Hartley Wilson and Bolt, and the builder was Andrewartha Bros. The agreed tender price was £4,749. A bank overdraft of £3,500 was secured and £800 came from the Sites Loans and Building Fund of the Home Mission. The Legion of donors gave £200 and a thank offering of £518 was given on the day.

Lenah Valley Baptist Church

Cordially invites you to the

Official Opening

of the

CHURCH HALL

2 POTTERY ROAD, LENAH VALLEY

on

SATURDAY, 26th NOVEMBER, 1960

at 3 p.m. by

Mr. IAN E. JOYCE

President of The Baptist Union of Tasmania

Architects: Builders:
HARTLEY WILSON & BOLT   ANDREWARTHA BROS.

Opening of Original Building – 26 Nov 1960

The completed sanctuary is a unique design, with a parabola-shaped front section which gives excellent acoustic qualities. It was written up in the Tasmanian Architect magazine in July 1961. The former ABC broadcaster, the late Ken Short, who came to speak once, was so impressed with the quality of sound in it, mainly due to the parabola-shape at one end, he said it would be a good building for sound recording. Some would remember the stylish architect designed wooden pews seating a total of fifty-six people. However, the seats were very hard to sit on, especially if the sermon was overly long! But the sanctuary was not designed for the future. Within a few years it was too small for the growing congregation. The fellowship had preferred an all-purpose hall which could easily be extended, but the Home Mission had other thoughts on the matter. In its view, since it held the purse strings, the sanctuary had to be worthy of the district; no cement sheets or weather boards were to be used to clad its exterior. The resulting clinker brick building was finished in 1960.

During its erection when young Charles Doran, a scholar at the Sunday school, asked the builders on the site what they were about, he was told that they were building an ice cream factory! On arriving home he excitedly informed his mother of this new venture on the church land. When the truth was revealed to this young mind, he courageously replied, "Oh, but I'm still going to Sunday School because if I go five Sundays, I will get a Bible." He received his sought-after Bible following his five weeks of attendance.

Opening of Original Building – 26 Nov 1960

The new building was opened by the President of the Baptist Union of Tasmania, Ian Joyce, on Saturday 26 November 1960. The key was presented by Mrs A Large who was the oldest member of the church at the time. There was a common thread to the stories of some who spoke on this opening day. The Hobart Baptist Tabernacle had been their spiritual home where they had both worshipped and served in its large Sunday school until the Sunday school commenced a branch in Lenah Valley. Yet the new building also proved inadequate for the large numbers of up to 130 Sunday school scholars attending so use was made of the Community Hall and, at times, the Primary School.

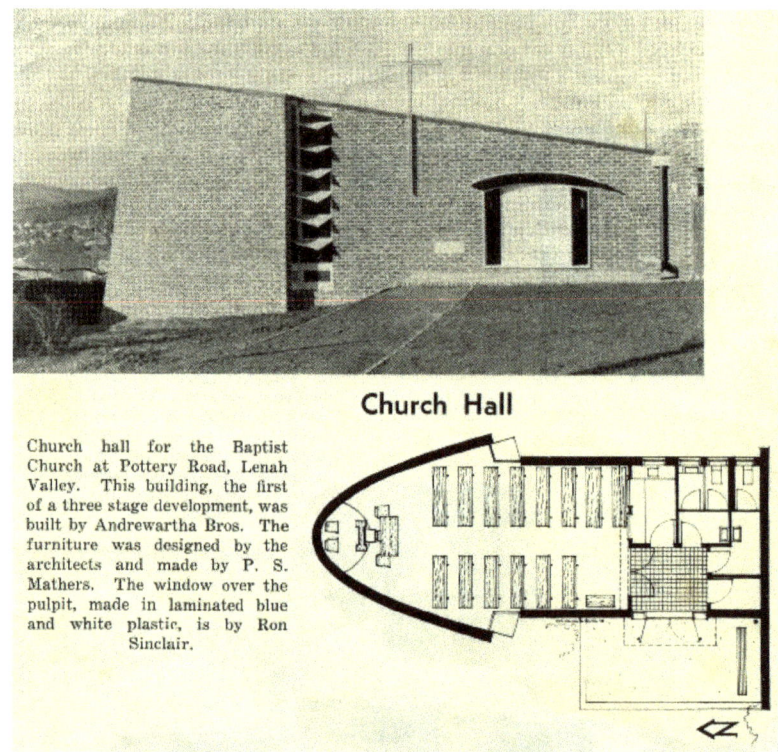

Church hall for the Baptist Church at Pottery Road, Lenah Valley. This building, the first of a three stage development, was built by Andrewartha Bros. The furniture was designed by the architects and made by P. S. Mathers. The window over the pulpit, made in laminated blue and white plastic, is by Ron Sinclair.

Architectural Drawing - Jul 1961

The opening of the building coincided with another children's mission, again conducted by Jack White and Warn's replacement, Donald Coleman. Their Mission ran from 29 November to 7 December 1960 and offered sound films, bright singing and thrilling stories.

A gowned youth choir of fourteen girls was formed during this time under the direction of Mrs Muriel Lawry. The choir sang at both the morning worship services and at other venues. They also appeared at the local TV station where they sang Christmas carols, and the recording was shown on TV in the weeks leading up to Christmas.

Building our Spiritual Home

During the ministry of Tom Green there were nine baptisms which were held at the Hobart Tabernacle for as yet there was no baptistery at Lenah Valley.

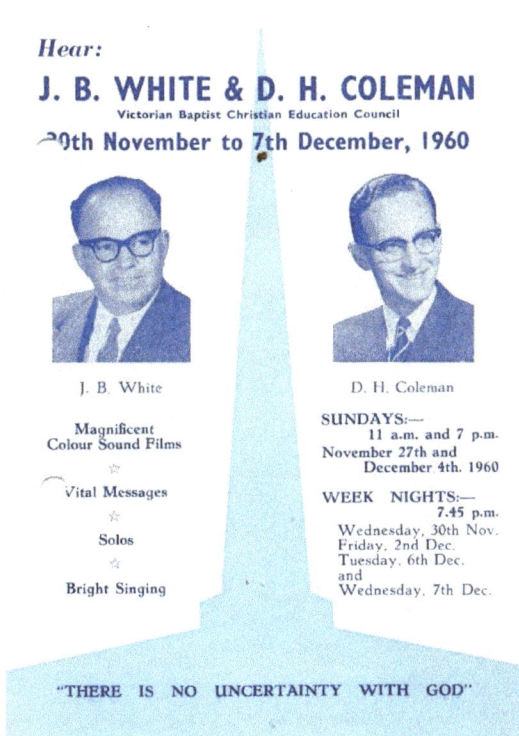

25

***Mr & Mrs Green's last service** – March 1961*

The Lenah Valley Baptist Church was constituted on 26 February 1961 with twenty-one foundation members, with sixteen transferring their memberships from the Hobart Tabernacle.

***Sunday School Picnic** – Blackmans Bay 1962*

Gowned Youth Choir – March 1961

Congregation - March 1961

Plaque on original lectern in memory of Thomas Kelly –1953

Lenah Valley Congregation –1978

Original Church Interior - Nov 1960

Dr Frank Kelly – 1952

Frank & Enid Kelly at Lenah Valley home - 1 Jan 1966

Kindergarten Sunday School Anniversary - Dec 1973

PASSING THE BATON

The Rev H. J. Martin Kerly

The Home Mission arranged for the Rev. Martin Kerly to commence on 7 May 1961 as an interim appointment for six months; he was transferring his allegiance from the Church of England and with his wife had been baptised at the Hobart Baptist Church. Martin Kerly became the church's first full time minister. During his time congregational numbers were maintained and at its conclusion, he was transferred to the pastorate of the Deloraine Baptist Church.

At the Annual Church Meeting on 15 August that year, the first diaconate for the Lenah Valley Baptist Church was elected comprising Jessie Seville, Enid Kelly, Frank Kelly, Andrew Lawry, Cliff Jacks and Maurice French. The average weekly attendance in 1961 was forty-seven people at the morning services and thirty at the evening services.

Pastor David Nibbs

Student Pastor David Nibbs was appointed to the church for January and February 1962. At the time he was between his college years at the Baptist College in Melbourne. There were four baptisms at the conclusion of his ministry. David Nibbs had been Pastor at the Elphin Road Baptist Church prior to his entry into College.

During this time Cliff Jacks arranged for a fibre glass

Pastor David Nibbs - 1962

baptistery to be installed in the rear corner of the church building and when a baptismal service occurred, the seating for the congregation was turned around to face the rear of the building.

By now renovation and extensions to provide sufficient accommodation in the original manse was financially out of the question. A house at 22 Suncrest Avenue, Lenah Valley came on the market and was purchased at auction in January 1962 for the sum of £6,600. The church took out a loan of £4,600 repayable over a period of twenty-five years and a short-term loan of £2,500 from the Home Mission. In April 1963, the original manse in Augusta Road was sold for £3,250 and all the short-term loans were repaid.

Pastor Allan R. Lehmann

In May 1962 A. Lehmann of Queensland, who was on extended furlough from the Borneo Evangelical Mission, commenced an interim appointment which was initially for three months but was extended to seven months. There was one baptism at the conclusion of this ministry.

Pastor & Mrs Lehman & Family *- Dec 1962*

Pastor David Nibbs

A second short term ministry by David Nibbs commenced in November 1962 and lasted until March the following year. There were two baptisms at the conclusion of this ministry.

David Nibbs transferred to the George Town Baptist Church until May 1964 when he resigned from the Tasmanian Baptist Churches finding himself in the school of thought which advocated Unconditional Election, a Limited Atonement and Irresistible Grace.

The Rev. Matthew Francis

Rev Matthew Francis - 1965

The house at 22 Suncrest Ave was rented out for a period. Members worked hard upgrading the interior and garden before the Francis family arrived from Shrewsbury, England.

In July 1962 the church secretary Dr Frank Kelly informed the members that Rev. Matthew Francis MA, B.Litt. was keen to move from England to Australia with his wife, Ruth, and their four children and that he was seeking pastoral employment. Finally, an invitation was issued by the church and accepted. The Home Mission which was not involved, accepted this decision.

The Church welcomed the family on 30 May 1963. Matthew Francis had a special interest in evangelism and the Torrey and Alexander evangelists who had come to Australia at the turn of the century. During his time, a young people's group and Junior and Intermediate Christian endeavour groups were commenced.

Matthew Francis became director of the Tasmanian Christian Television Association and a number of its congregational hymn singing programmes were filmed in the Church. A Carol Singing session, also filmed in the building, was broadcasted on radio 7HO.

Rod Tedds who had recently arrived from England in January 1965 became the church organist. He was taken by the smallness of the building. Rod was a teacher at New Town High School in 1965 and in 1966 moved to The Friends' School, North Hobart. In 1970 the family became adherents at the Moonah Salvation Army Corps prior to joining the Sandy Bay Baptist Church in 1972. In 1987, Rod became the Principal of Riverstone Christian Community School, Riverstone, NSW, before returning to a similar position at Calvin Christian School, Kingston, in 1992, when Rod and his wife Pearl returned to Lenah Valley Baptist Church.

Rev Matthew & Ruth Francis, Matthew, Timothy, Margaret and Anna - 1962

In 1965 Matthew Francis gave the sermon for the opening of State Parliament. After three years, the family transferred to a Baptist Church in South Perth, WA.

The Rev. Don Leslie Johnson

The Rev Matthew Francis was followed by the Rev. Don Johnson who had just completed his studies at the Baptist College of NSW. He was inducted on 5 February 1967. Earlier a widower, he was accompanied by his new wife Margaret. Don Johnson became known as the "egg man" as each week he would deliver eggs from the egg farm in upper Pottery Road to folk in the church.

Don Johnson was ordained at the Hobart Baptist Church on 11 August 1967. In Hobart he became Director of Youth for Christ. At Lenah Valley, Don Johnson ran a yearly camp at Conningham for the young people of the church's Christian Endeavour Society.

Church Youth Camp at Carton - late 1968

The church held annual Sunday school picnics at different locations. Maurice French had his boat at the Dodges Ferry picnic one year when they did some water skiing. He remembers Don Johnson wanting to have a try at water skiing. After some basic instructions on technique, he was ready to give it a go. Don was told to hang on and the boat would pull him up out of the water. Don did hang on, but all that could be seen was a great wave of water following the boat. After a few seconds it was realised that he was not going to come up on the skis so the boat was stopped and Don popped up spluttering a lot and said, "You told me to hang on and I did!" It was probably his last try at water skiing.

In 1968, the church farewelled Dr Frank Kelly and his wife Enid and one of their daughters for their new life in Singapore.

Frank had been a senior lecturer in applied chemistry at the University of Tasmania before his appointment as professor of applied chemistry at the University of Singapore. Frank was the son of Tasmanian Baptist missionaries, the Rev. Thomas Churchward-Kelly and his wife Stella (nee Churchward) who served from 1915 in Sirajganj, India. The original architect-designed pulpit made for the opening of the new church building in 1960, has a plaque on it in memory of Rev Thomas-Churchward Kelly.

Don Johnson's ministry at Lenah Valley concluded in May 1971.

The Rev. Don C. Cameron

In 1973, after seven years in Victoria, Don Cameron returned for a ministry at the joint Moonah and Lenah Valley pastorate, commencing 18 February 1973. During this joint pastorate, the work stalled after he suffered an accident when he was knocked over by a car. He had to take twenty-three weeks off work due to severe back injuries. In his three years at the joint pastorate, he represented the British and Foreign Bible Society and the Hobart Branch of the Tasmanian Council of Churches. He also served for a time both on the state committee for the ABMS and the Baptist Union Church Extension Committee.

Rev Don Cameron - 1973

At Lenah Valley a new building extension on the front of the property, on the right hand side, was carried out to cater for the Sunday school and other meetings.

Building extension, Doug & Ruth Williams – Oct 1982

Further Tasmanian Baptist pastorates followed for Don Cameron after the three years at the joint Moonah and Lenah Valley pastorate and in the midst of these he served as an I.T.I.M. Chaplain serving the Hydro Electric Commission at Tarraleah. He retired in 1995.

Active Church Membership in July 1974 was twenty-four. In October that year, after many years of faithful service, foundation member Andrew Lawry retired both as Church Secretary and diaconate member.

On 28 May 1977 the official opening of the new hall of the property took place; it a cost of $20,000.

Pastor Jim T. Yeo

A pastorless period of two years followed and ended with the induction of Jim Yeo from NSW in June 1978. He had just concluded three years of study at the Tahlee Bible College in NSW. The College Principal arranged for him to come as a worker Pastor.

He was married in 1978 and the church welcomed his wife Denise. He found the church to be an enthusiastic group of young families with a large Sunday school and a large and active youth group. Martyn Whitley ran the youth group. Martyn was a single man who

Pastor Jim and Denise Yeo - 1979

was employed part time in the Public service. He gave considerable time to leadership of the youth group and was involved in the establishing of a Christian FM Radio station in Hobart. During Jim Yeo's time a good number of past Sunday school and youth group members continued in fellowship with the church and were baptised.

Church Membership numbers rose to 35 in 1978/79 and to 41 for the 1979/80 year. In December 1979 Jim Yeo concluded his

ministry and commenced full-time ministerial training in March 1980 at the Baptist Theological College in Queensland.

On 20 December 1979 the Lenah Valley manse at 22 Suncrest Avenue was sold for $40,000 to enable in faith a full-time minister to be called.

Ken Godfrey, Simon Sircar & Hans Bohm - Oct 1982

Early in 1980 the Rev. Ken Godfrey joined in membership at the church and was appointed moderator. He had just concluded a ministry at the George Town Baptist Church.

Sunday School with Stamp Shield – Feb 1980

THE BOHM BOOM

The Rev Hans J. Bohm

On 15 February 1981 the Rev. Hans Bohm, BTh., DipTheol., was inducted into the pastorate with a membership of fifty with five members being on the non-resident roll. At the time at Sunday morning services there was an average of fifty in attendance and twenty-five on average in the Sunday evenings. During his four years the church experienced unprecedented and remarkable growth as he preached in an uncompromising way. This was seen in the thirty-four baptisms as people responded to the claims of Jesus Christ and testified to the change that had taken place in their lives. The membership rose to seventy-nine and attendance at the morning service increased to 130 people. A number of people transferred their memberships from other churches.

Rev Hans & Sheila Bohm - Dec 1984

Many other positive things happened during this time. Prayers were answered as the folk prayed for young couples to come, and they came, and in due course newborns started arriving. There were at least eleven infant dedications in the wake of this "baby boom".

In July 1981 services were moved to the new hall and when this was full-to-overflowing, the church commenced two morning services. This proved unsuccessful so the decision was taken to enlarge the hall to the current worship centre size. During construction, the church met in the Community Hall.

Sheila, Ian, Hans & Stacy Bohm

The construction over twelve months was done mainly by church members under the direction of John Drummond. Every Saturday and public holidays were taken up with working bees, while the excavations, the structural steel framing, bricklaying, electrical wiring and plumbing were all sub-contracted. It was built at a cost of $40,000. On 20 May 1984 the church held its first service in the enlarged auditorium and four baptisms took

Excavating the foundations for the new auditorium - Nov 1983

place in the new baptistery under the front stage. The project was officially opened in July 1984. The auditorium now had a seating capacity for about 130 people. The original clinker brick building on the rear of the block was allocated to a multi-purpose hall.

Outreach in the community was strengthened by Friendship Days when elderly folk met together on a regular basis for lunch and an enjoyable and varied programme. This ministry was initiated by Hans Bohm's wife Sheila and supported by the Ladies' Fellowship. It celebrated the 30th Anniversary on 21 July 1984 with about forty women attending.

Installing the roof on the new auditorium – 30 March 1984

Hans Bohm prepared several series of Bible study notes for use by the study groups, and he held regular training sessions on how to lead these groups. A pastoral team was also formed. Hans Bohm's own visitation method was unique. He would visit mostly unannounced, saying that he was just calling for ten minutes. He lived by the adage: "a home visiting pastor means a church attending people".

He served for a year as a chaplain at the St Ann's Nursing Home. He was also Vice Chairman and then Chairman of the Baptist Union Church Extension Committee.

In October 1983 a deacons' retreat was held to consider the aims and strategies of the Church. The Church welcomed two visits from American Lay Renewal Teams which proved a blessing and challenge to all.

Sheila Bohm worked nights as a nursing sister to pay off the mortgage of the house they had purchased in the suburb. During these four years Hans Bohm worked on a Doctorate of Ministry under the supervision of the Christian Baptist University of Louisiana, USA.

On 28 July 1984 the new enlarged church auditorium was opened. Church membership had now risen to 80 people with about 130 attending morning services.

Hans concluded his Tasmanian ministry 2 December 1984 and moved to Bracken Ridge in Brisbane.

Member Leonie Fyffe was farewelled as she departed to study at the Bible College in Sydney.

Ladies Fellowship - 30th Anniversary - 21 July 1984

The Rev. Ken and Margaret Godfrey also departed as Ken became Associate Pastor of the Hobart Baptist Church.

Associate Pastor Les J. Maus

During Hans Bohm's ministry, the Church had the benefit of an Associate Pastor in Les Maus, who, with his English born wife Alyn, focused on the youth work; they had recently married. They were both recent graduates of the NSW Baptist College. They were welcomed on 14 March 1982 and stayed until the end of 1983. With his induction one member commented, "We meet in a church which we thought we couldn't afford, and have two pastors when we thought we couldn't afford one."

Les & Alyn Maus - 1982

Les Maus was born in Melbourne and attended the Aberfeldie Baptist Church with Hans Bohm as Pastor. He came to faith in 1975 and took on the church's youth work. Later he was appointed youth worker at Turramurra Baptist Church in NSW.

American Lay Renewal Team outside Church - 22 May 1983

In December 1984 the church bought a house at 22 Sharps Rd for future use as a manse. It was rented out until a future pastor arrived.

The Clarke's on a church family picnic- 1990

Carlos Cruz - Praise be to God
2012 Acrylic on 3mm MDF (40cm x 60cm)

The scene symbolises the power of His light and the joy when one receives it. When I first came to know about Jesus I was in a dark place, but I didn't know how dark it was until I followed that glimmer of hope. That shaft of light that can reach anyone no matter where they are or where they've been. With God, nothing is impossible. Praise be to God. (Extract from Prison Fellowship Australia (Tasmania))

Ladies' Meeting Fun Night – weddings through the ages - 1992

AN ON-GOING TIME OF MINISTRY

The Rev Malcolm Eberhard

On 2 February 1986 the Rev. Malcolm Eberhard from the Salem Baptist Church, Gumeracha, SA, was inducted into the pastorate and stayed for five years. At Gumeracha, Malcolm had become actively involved in community and sporting groups. His emphasis on teaching led to teaching missions at schools as well as a teaching mission in the Solomon Islands.

Induction of Rev Malcolm Eberhard. Des Richardson, John Ryall, Malcolm Eberhard, Martyn Whiteley & Maurice French – Feb 1986

In 1988 the church enjoyed the month-long ministry of two "Summer Missionaries" from Texas. Early that year evening worship services ceased as there were now "home church" meetings conducted on Sunday afternoons and evenings. At the time John Ryall, who was church secretary, became President of the Baptist Union for 1988/89.

Over these years the youth group grew considerably under the leadership of Martyn Whiteley. Martyn, a keen Christian and gifted leader, bought a Volkswagen Combi to transport the youth group.

Milk Carton Race at Longford – Mar 1986

At one petrol stop, the youngsters leaned out the windows calling, "Daddy, daddy can we have ice-creams!" Martyn commenced a weekly homework time which proved extremely popular for the young people. The neighbour, Professor Beresford from the UTAS Mathematics Department and now retired, assisted. Fundraising activities at the time to pay off the debt included car washes, lamington drives (when the church hall floor enjoyed a covering of coconut), mystery car rallies, picnics, camps and amazing craft evenings.

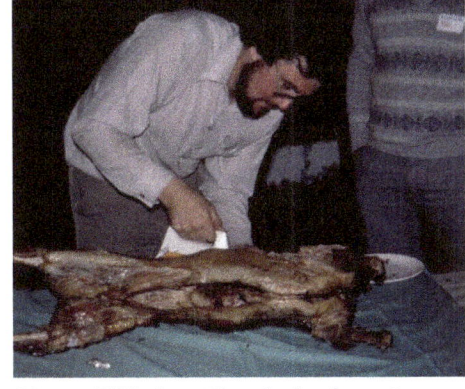

Martyn Whitely cutting the lamb roast – March 1980

Pastor Peter Matthewson

Peter Matthewson

On 16 February 1991 Peter Matthewson who had been involved with Tasmanian Baptists at Longford and Devonport and with the Assemblies of God at Latrobe and Devonport, and having gained a Certificate of Ministry course from the Assembly of God Bible School, was inducted into the pastorate. Peter was on leave from the Education Department having sensed a call to full-time Christian ministry among Tasmanian Baptists. He and his wife Judith concluded at the end of 1992.

The Rev Gary Piper

The Rev. Gary Piper began a three-month interim ministry on 19 April 1993. He and his wife, Rosemary, were on leave from Australian Baptist Missionary Society (ABMS).

Early in their time at Lenah Valley they ran a congregational dinner as part of the visitation programme. Gary aimed to visit each church member twice a year and while on visitation Gary would ask, "What would you be excited and passionate about doing in terms of ministry?" Soon Rod Tedds was appointed as the first Elder. There were bi-monthly luncheons, SHAPE seminars, study groups, home prayer groups, Monday nights' Adventure Club for children seven to fourteen years with up to thirty attending, a Sunday school with ten scholars (which grew to seventeen) and a weekly weekday morning prayer group. In 1995 another two "Summer Missionaries" spent a month at the church.

By Gary's third year he had taken upon himself the running of a total of ten Bible study groups each month. A bi-weekly morning craft group commenced. Both the Covenant Players and French's Forest Bell Ringers visited. By the end of the Piper's time, the membership stood at thirty-five.

During his time Gary also ministered as a chaplain with the Army Reserve Unit at 10th Field Ambulance at Dowsing Point.

Gary died on 22 June 2009 aged 51 years. A full Military Funeral for Lieutenant Colonel (Rev) Gary Piper was held on 30 June 2009 at the Diamond Valley Baptist Church, Plenty, Victoria.

Rev Gary Piper – April 1993

The Rev Paul D Kerrison

The Rev Paul Kerrison, B.Th., Dip.Min, began at Lenah Valley on 12 February 1999. He commenced part-time on twenty hours a week. For the other half of the week, he worked as a builder and joiner. He became the longest serving pastor over the life of the church. His term commenced with the church having a membership of thirty, a Sunday school of twelve scholars, three Bible study groups, nine youngsters in the youth group, the manse rented out, luncheons after Sunday morning church, games nights, the first of a number of Alpha Courses and a church camp.

Elder Rod Tedds took on the task of Church Secretary. When three families departed in Paul's second year, the Sunday school disbanded as it was nearly unviable and the youth group was depleted. The children's work took the form of a "Children's FunZone". Yet church functions continued, among them barbecues and progressive dinners. A "Playgroup" for young mothers commenced. The Baptist youth from the various Hobart churches formed a network, Lenah Valley included. One family involved itself in a church planting venture at Bridgewater. It was decided to sell the manse at 22 Sharps Rd as each pastor now preferred to purchase his own home.

Lenah Valley welcomes Paul Kerrison

On 12 February Paul Kerrison was inducted into the pastorate of the Lenah Valley Church. Paul was born on the West Tamar in 1952, the third son of godly Methodist parents. His formative years were spent on the family orchard, near Exeter. He attended the Exeter Area School and on leaving found employment as an apprentice carpenter and joiner in Launceston. His early church experience was in the Methodist Church at Supply River and Exeter where he was confirmed. Later as a teenager he gave his life to Christ.

"My personal commitment came as a result of being woken from deep sleep late one night by the Lord," says Paul, "who prompted me to read Revelation 3:20: 'Here I am! I stand at the door and knock. If anyone hears my voice and opens the door, I will come in and eat with him, and he with me.' I realised that up until that time I had not invited Christ into my life as Lord and Saviour."

In the following years Paul attended the Margaret Street Church of Christ in Launceston, eventually being involved with youth groups and Christian Endeavour.

At the completion of his apprenticeship he moved to Hobart and started as a building contactor and later as a real estate salesman with Hank Petrusma-Tony Williams Real Estate. He was involved in youth and later small group leadership positions within the life of the Collins Street Church of Christ and later the Howah Church of Christ prior to accepting the call of God to train for pastoral ministry.

He trained in Sydney at the Churches of Christ (N.S.W.) Theological College (Carlingford) 1984-1987, graduating with a Diploma of Ministry and a Bachelor of Theology. He is currently doing a Post Graduate

(Continued on page 2)

In his third year, the church extended Paul Kerrison's engagement to four days a week. That year, there were a number of farewells and the membership stood at twenty-five, yet with the closure of the Moonah Baptist Church in 2003, twenty new folk were seen at the Lenah Valley services.

Paul, the Pastor/builder, proposed a multi-purpose room and entrance porch be added and these extensions were completed by the end of 2005. He used his many skills and installed a high-quality sound system in the church. A "40 days of Purpose" seminar was held in 2004.

An Ongoing Time of Ministry

Paul Kerrison – Nov 2011

By 2004, member Wanda King was conducting holiday bus tours across Tasmania, as well as interstate, under the designation, "The Mobile Munchers".

In 2005 two members, Charles Wressell and his wife Valerie departed to study at Morling College in Sydney.

Southern Baptist Convention American missionaries resident in Hobart, the Rev. Ben and Judy Armacost, contributed to church life.

Citywide Baptist Church - one church, two locations, 2008 Rev John & Heather Smith, Rev Paul & Elizabeth Kerrison

ONE CHURCH TWO LOCATIONS

During Paul Kerrison's time at Lenah Valley many discussions were held regarding the Lenah Valley Church joining with the Citygate Baptist Church at Mornington on the Eastern Shore. The idea was to become one church in two locations. So on 6 April 2008, the merger took place and officially the Lenah Valley complex became Citywide Baptist Church (Lenah Valley) since a renaming took place. The church at Mornington became Citywide Baptist Church (Mornington). This merger was not something entered into lightly, but once the decision was made, both churches have been blessed in many ways.

Andy & Muriel Lawry in original church auditorium - 23 Dec 2013

In 2011 Maurice French stepped down as elder having given fifty years of leadership. Many years earlier he had been appointed to the first diaconate. Following the merger, Maurice became the Finance Officer of Citywide Baptist Church, a position he held for 10 years.

In 2013 the Lenah Valley Church was conducting a monthly service at the nearby Roy Fagan Centre.

Paul Kerrison concluded his ministry at Lenah Valley in July 2012 when he joined the leadership team of Citywide Baptist Church.

Siegfried and Ruth's 60th wedding anniversary 12 Sept 2010

In 2007 a German couple, Siegfried and Ruth Strohbach, had joined the church and on their deaths left a lasting legacy to the Lenah Valley Baptist Church. Their early story, like that of Rev Hans Bohm, is quite harrowing. They were married after the Second World War while they were in an East German Russian controlled camp. Instead of celebrating with a wedding reception, they were given an extra dollop of custard for their dessert! They escaped on a push bike and eventually immigrated to Australia; they had no family. When the Lenah Valley church put on a luncheon complete with a specially iced cake to celebrate their golden wedding anniversary, it was the first celebratory cake they had ever been given. Siegfried was fluent in about thirteen languages as was Ruth, but Ruth's health was poor and she died on 1 July 2012; Siegfried died less than a month later on 27 July.

Siegfried bequeathed the whole of their estate to the Lenah Valley Baptist Church. After a tithe was given to Christian work that the Strobach's had supported, the balance was used firstly to upgrade the Lenah Valley Church building and furnishings and at Mornington, its property debt of $215,000, was cleared. The church had a headstone erected at the Cornelian Bay Cemetery in their memory.

Peter Clarke with his wife Barbara joined the church in 1982. He became a deacon and then an elder. On the merger of the two congregations, Peter served as an elder over both campuses and then chairman of elders. With failing health, he died on 5 October 2022 after years of lovable, prayerful and dedicated service. His memorial service was held at Citywide Mornington on 12 October 2022 with an attendance of about 350 people.

Peter Clarke cutting the 60th Birthday Cake - 2016

The Rev John Smith

The Rev. John Smith and his wife Heather moved from the Mount Gambier Church in SA. to take the lead at the Eastern Shore Church in 2002. John was inducted in 15 December 2002. Their call to the Eastern Shore/Citywide Church was a sort of "man from Macedonia" situation.

Rev John and Heather Smith – Dec 2002

With the merger of the two churches in April 2008, John Smith continued in his role as Senior Pastor. The merger took place after a year of discussion, planning and the development of a memorandum of understanding. Both churches employed the services of Rev Dr David Jones, a respected Baptist pastor and church consultant, to help in the process.

Maddy & Imogen Svoboda - Mar 2015

Seven years later, on a half time basis, John Smith took on the additional responsibility as leader of the Mission Leadership Team of Tasmanian Baptists. He retired as Senior Pastor of Citywide Baptist Church at the end of April 2015, yet continued as Superintendent of Tasmanian Baptists and undertook an interim ministry with Riverlands, the Longford Baptist Church. Now in retirement in South Australia, he continues to work with churches and pastors, in mentoring and ministry supervision as the Lord leads.

In 2014 the Rev Maddy Svoboda who had been youth pastor at the Citywide Mornington campus was given Pastoral oversight of the Lenah Valley congregation for a time before he and his wife, Imogen, left to pastor the Summerhill Church in Launceston.

Baptism service - 2014

The Rev Dr David Roffe

The Rev. David Roffe was appointed interim Senior Pastor for Citywide Baptist Church in May 2015 initially for nine months as the church sought a replacement senior pastor. He was joined by his wife Joy. The church was greatly blessed by David's ministry and guidance over this transition period which was extended to become two years with his hours increased to four days a week.

Andrew Lawry, one of the founders of the Lenah Valley church, died on 26 August 2016. His funeral service, led by Paul Kerrison, was held at the Citywide Lenah Valley Baptist church with about 100 people attending. Andrew Lawry on leaving the Baptists, had returned to his original Presbyterian fold.

Dr David Roffe – Nov 2015

STRETCHING OUR TENT PEGS – WELCOMING THE NEPALESE

The Nepalese Fellowship

Lenah Valley Nepalese and English-speaking congregations - 2011

The Church a little over a decade ago was made aware of a growing refugee group of Nepalese Christians in Southern Tasmania and arrangements were made to collect individuals from their homes to join the Lenah Valley worship services. The Lenah Valley folk were never quite sure just how many would be at a particular house, but they realised that many had a real passion for Jesus Christ and were keen to evangelise other Nepalese in Hobart.

In June 2011 the Nepalese began meeting once a month with the folk at the Lenah Valley Church in the morning services, but they also held Nepalese Sunday afternoon services in their Pastor Paul Rai's

Maddy Svoboda & Suraj Darjee - Dec 2014

garage in Moonah. This Nepalese Christian community had commenced with just two families.

When the Lenah Valley congregation heard of their need for more seating the church gave them their bench seating as they were not needed due to a renovation and upgrade.

Nepalese Christmas Service - 2014

In 2012 the Nepalese people were invited by Pastor John Smith to use the Lenah Valley Campus for their services as they had outgrown the garage space. This led to them having ministry together with the Lenah Valley congregation.

At times, some of the Nepalese men would go back to Nepal to marry and return with their new wives. Thus the Nepalese numbers grew.

By 2015 the Nepalese comprised ten families numbering about forty persons including children. The fellowship was running a cottage (house) meeting, a women's fellowship, a fasting Prayer Chain on Saturdays once a month, a Sunday Kids' class, a Sunday afternoon service and humanitarian work. As an evangelistic venture, Pastor Rai was offering free driving lessons to Nepalese people in Hobart.

Stretching Our Tent Pegs

Nepalese Christmas Service - 2014

The Nepalese Fellowship formally joined as another congregation of the Citywide Baptist Church in 2017. Pastor Suraj Darjee, a graduate from the University of Tasmania, then joined Pastor Rai in the work. Pastor Darjee and his family eventually moved to Albury, NSW, where he worked as a pharmacist.

In 2020 the Nepalese Fellowship was constituted as Citywide Hobart Nepalese Church. The Nepalese Community continues to function similar to the way that the Christian Church in Australia functioned one hundred years ago; that is, their church is both the Nepalese community centre and the House of God. Sadly, for Australians today, Sunday church is now no longer a community centre, just the House of God, one of the many "entertainments" available on the Lord's Day.

Pastor Paul Rai

Paul was born in Bhutan and moved to Nepal in 1992 as a refugee after the Nepalese people were forced to leave Bhutan. He lived in Nepal as a refugee for 14 years.

In 2003 he became a Christian along with his family and at the

Aaron, Manisha, Aiden & Paul - 2022

age of 17 felt called by God to undertake theological studies which he did in India from 2004 to 2007.

Paul graduated from Asian Mission Seminary in India in 2006.

Paul came to Australia under a humanitarian visa in 2010 and in the same year established the first Nepalese church in Tasmania as the Hobart Nepali Church. The church met in Paul's garage for 2 years.

Pastor Paul Rai officially became a pastor of Citywide Baptist Church on 4 March 2018. He is the pastor for the Nepalese congregation that meets at the Lenah Valley Campus.

The Rev Matt Garvin

On 10 July 2017 Tasmanian, the Rev. Matt Garvin replaced David Roffe.

Josh, Matt, Dan, Leeanne, Sophie and Maddi Garvin - 2017

In 2018 the Lenah Valley church celebrated its 70th anniversary with a special afternoon tea with a cake that was cut by Mrs Muriel Lawry who was the oldest remaining worshipper at the Church. The senior photographer from the Mercury newspaper there that day to take a photograph for the next day's edition, whispered to his junior offsider, "Don't muck it up, her husband was the Manager of the paper for many years." For the occasion a timeline of the church's history was erected along the wall of the auditorium as a focal point for all the invited past and present members to share their stories.

Muriel Lawry cutting the Anniversary Cake - 2018

Over many years as a further outreach, the church has been supporting five children through Baptist World Aid. After a visit by member Agnes Webb to an orphanage in Zambia, it was unanimously agreed that the church add five more children to the list, to make a total of ten children the church is supporting from a special offering each week.

Early in Mat Garvin's ministry, Mornington and Lenah Valley congregations were linked by an on-line video network so the worship service could be shared between the two campuses. The worship service was also broadcast on YouTube so a wider number of people could join in the service. This technology was invaluable when the COVID-19 pandemic struck, as it was adapted to enable the congregations to continue to meet via Zoom even though they couldn't meet in the same physical location.

Lenah Valley Congregation - Nov 2017

Executive Pastor Dan Evenhuis

Tasmanian born Dan Evenhuis and his wife Danni and their four children migrated from the UK in 2021 after 18 years of ministry with Fusion UK and OpenDoors. Dan began working as Executive Pastor at Citywide from 30 Jan 2022.

Dan, Josiah, Danni, Simeon, Anya & Bridie - 2022

*Kitchen Upgrade –
Nov 2013*

*Agnes Webb and Maurice French -
2013*

*Baptisimal Service -
Lenah Valley
- 14 Dec 2014*

Nepalese Christmas Service 2014

Youth Service Lenah Valley
- 22 Nov 2015

Matt Garvin farewelling Bill & Deidre Smith
- 18 Nov 2018

Dianne Allen - Membership - 14 Dec 2014

Ruth Ridley's 80th Birthday & Judy Clifford - 17 Apr 2016

Glenn Giffard at Baptisimal Service -14 Dec 2014

Eunice Darjee Birthday & Dedication - 11 Dec 2016

75 YEARS AND COUNTING

A brief glimpse at this book quickly reveals that Lenah Valley's Baptist church has avoided the stagnation that besets many older congregations. It seems every five years or so the church has reinvented itself, seeking to find new ways to serve its community.

It is clear that there have been at least three decisive moments in its trajectory.

The first decisive moment was the choice to plant the church with a Sunday school for local children. One of those original children is still a part of this church today.

The second was when the church risked everything to employ Hans Bohm, knowing the decision could be its demise. As the book indicates, the 'Bohm Boom' bore great fruit.

The third decisive moment was the choice to partner with two other congregations rather than remain self-focussed.

The open-hearted welcome the congregation gave the Nepalese church planted by Paul Rai was unusual at the time, but resulted in the single biggest number of new members added to a Baptist church in Tasmania by any one church when the whole congregation joined as members in March 2018.

The other Congregational partnership, with what was then Citygate Baptist, was perhaps even more radical than welcoming the Nepalese. In forming one new church across two campuses, the smaller Lenah Valley congregation showed incredible humility as their finances helped pay off the bigger church's debt and yet often felt as though they didn't get enough attention from the church's leaders who were stretched across both sites.

The dilemma of the two sites eventually forced a technological solution which meant that Citywide Baptist church was ready to quickly pivot during the COVID pandemic and host online church services for smaller Baptist churches across the state.

So what's next?

As reading this book will have shown you, there has not been a point at which Lenah Valley's Baptist church was predictable, so trying to predict where the church will be in twenty-five years is impossible.

One thing though is predictable. If Citywide Lenah Valley continues to serve its local community and to seek partnership in the way it has, it will continue to make surprising and life-giving changes. It's worth remembering that many of the people who in the future will call it their church family have quite possibly not even heard of it yet.

Just as many of the Baptist churches in Tasmania benefitted from the technological trailblazing of Lenah Valley leading up to the pandemic, many individuals will also benefit from the faithful stewardship of the those who have served so faithfully over the past seventy-five years. Whether they know it or not, many will continue to be blessed by the foundation laid since the 1st of August 1948.

Lenah Valley Garage Sale – 2 Apr 2011

Some of those we have loved and lost.

Watermelon Race, ANZAC Day at John Turnbull Park - 2022

ANZAC Day at John Turnbull Park - 2022

Rodney Dale cutting a birthday cake with Barbie Clarke.

Dale Herbert and Paul Banham working on the PA – Mar 2021

Celebrating a birthday in the rear hall.

Clean Up Australia Day at Creek Rd, Moonah - 2022

Jean Walker with Vasile Mocean from Romania - Nov 2012

Dan and Maree Hutcherson at MAANS - Dec 2021

Andy Lawry & Maurice French - 20 Dec 2013

Wednesday Prayer and Healing - 2022

Post-Sunday Service Lunch at Grenada Tavern - 2022

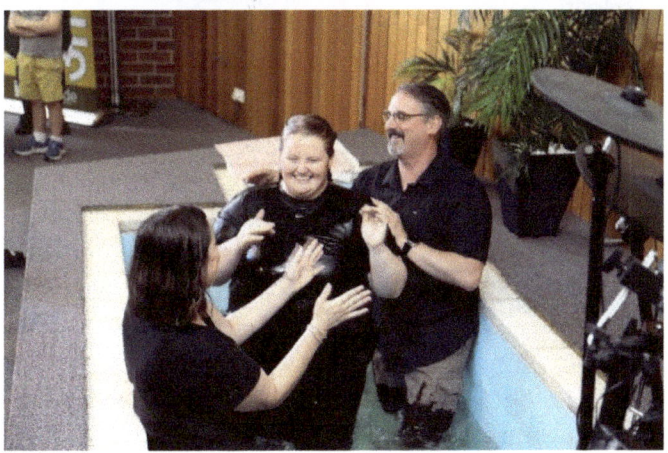

Sophie Griffiths Baptism with Emily McCormack and Dan Evenhuis – 19 Feb 2023

APPENDICES – VARIOUS PASTORS' HISTORIES

The Rev John Toroni

The Rev Toroni returned to NSW in 1951 with his Australian wife Eunice to conduct missions among the churches; he was by now a distinguished violinist. In America he had performed with the Philadelphia Symphony Orchestra and toured the states in theatrical work. There he turned down several offers of contracts and applied himself to his Gospel preaching. While on the Christian missions in NSW, Eunice took an active part as pianist and soloist. As Rev Toroni preached, he often played the violin to "emphasise the spoken word", thus the phrase, "the speaking violin". The newspapers reported that he could describe some incident such as a storm and then produce its sound effects on his violin. He could also imitate a fighter plane dogfight, and animal and bird sounds, and give an impression of a mouse being caught in a trap. On their Australian tour he said, "I am in this country to introduce the sacred concert in various churches". He established several church orchestras in NSW as he challenged young people to use their talents to worship God.

The Rev Trevor Fist

Trevor Fist was born on 4 October 1925, the first of six children to Methodists Albert Gladstone and Elsie Jane Fist. They farmed at Milabena and later at Boat Harbour in the Table Cape district in the North West of Tasmania. For a time his mother was organist at the Myalla Church, an outstation of the Wynyard Baptist Church. As a boy at Milabena he also attended the Myalla Gospel Hall. In his late teens Trevor was part of the Young People's Groups at both the Boat Harbour Baptist Church and the Wynyard Methodist Church.

Trevor preached in the local Methodist churches in the Wynyard/Yolla circuit until as a candidate for the Methodist ministry he entered Melbourne Bible Institute for the 1947 year. His friend Trevor Waite, a Baptist from Wynyard, also attended the College for a very short time in 1948. But through his years of study, Trevor's views changed and he became convinced of the duty and privilege of believer's baptism.

In 1949, he spent some months as a Victorian Baptist Home Missionary in Traralgon, a placement which was followed by studies to gain his matriculation. Early in 1950 he entered training at the NSW Baptist College and was student pastor at Chester Hill Baptist Church, Sydney. On 24 February 1954 he was ordained in the Burnie Baptist Church. At this time Trevor married June Waite who had attended the Baptist Training Institute in Melbourne training to be a deaconess in preparation for life as a Baptist minister's wife. For them the joint South Hobart-Lenah Valley pastorate followed.

The Rev Tom Green

Tom Green was born in Launceston on 23 June 1923. At the age of eighteen, he came to Christian faith and was baptised in the Launceston Tabernacle. At that time he was employed by the Tasmanian Education Department as a Laboratory Assistant in the Electrical Engineering Section of the Launceston Technical College.

In January 1942 he entered the Australian Army and was assigned to the Signals Branch as an electrician and radio technician. He served in New Guinea for a couple of years, rising to the rank of Sergeant. At the time of his discharge in December 1946, he was a staff instructor in radio at the Balcombe School of Signals in Victoria.

He returned to Launceston and with financial assistance from the Defence Rehabilitation Scheme, continued his Electrical

Engineering studies and pursued additional matriculation studies. In 1948 he undertook his ministerial training at the Victorian Baptist Theological College, gaining a LTh. He was ordained in the Launceston Central Baptist Church, having been inducted into the pastorate of the Wynyard Baptist Church. After the Wynyard ministry he accepted the call to the Hobart Church. Following his time at Lenah Valley, further pastorates took place at the Smithton Church, at the Wynyard Church for a second time, the Moonah Church with oversight of the South Hobart Church, then the Carina Church in Queensland.

Rev Don Johnson

English born Don Johnson had migrated from England in 1957. He worked as a French wood polisher and became a registered male nurse serving at St. John's Park, New Town. He served in the army in Korea and Japan as a medical orderly. He had been associated with the Gospel Hall in Burnie and the Sandy Bay and Moonah Baptist churches. Don Johnson had held an honorary pastorate at George Town from June to December 1962 before he transferred to North Auburn Baptist Church, WA.

Rev Don Cameron

Don Cameron was twenty-one when he came to Christian faith under the ministries of an American evangelist and the Rev. Alec White. He then studied at the Melbourne Bible Institute. He became the first Home Mission Pastor of the newly formed Marrawah and District Baptist Fellowship in the north-west of the State. Adelaide followed where he commenced studies at the South Australian Baptist College and this involved student pastorates. He was ordained in 1960 as he served at the Penguin Baptist Church in Tasmania. His next placement was at the joint Somerset-Yolla pastorate. Seven years in Victoria followed, as he accepted a call from the Lilydale and Wandin North Baptist churches. Then there was Morwell Baptist Church in the Latrobe Valley.

Jim Yeo

Jim Yeo grew up on a farm in central NSW near Wellington. The Principal of the Tahlee Bible College which he was attending at the time arranged for him to go to Lenah Valley as a worker Pastor. While connected to the Baptist College in Queensland after his time at Lenah Valley, he was pastor in a church planting situation at Burpengary for three years. He then had twelve months interim ministry at his original church at Wellington. His next pastorate, commencing in February 1984, was in the remote, hot, dry "frontier" mining town of Cobar, 711 kilometres from Sydney. The fellowship was part of Home Mission ministries of Western District Baptist Association. There the membership doubled in the first twelve months and the church was constituted. He was ordained on 13 October 1985. Further pastorates took place in Carnarvon, WA, and Mudgee, NSW.

In his final years of employment he worked for fifteen years in Group homes as a disability support worker in Dubbo and then retired. He and Denise are now part of the Orana Baptist Church and works the farm he had long left behind.

Rev Dr Hans Bohm

Hans Bohm was just ten years old and living in East Germany when the Lenah Valley Sunday school began. By the age of eleven he was living in London working as a barrow boy. A position of fireman followed in Kent. He married English born Sheila who lived in Surrey. They migrated to Melbourne in 1967 and both came to Christian faith under the ministry of the Rev. Alan Nunn at the Doveton Baptist Church. Hans responded to God's call to full-time service. Both Hans and Sheila spent two years at the Melbourne Bible Institute and thereafter for Hans, three years at Whitley Baptist Theological College. Following ministries with the Baptist Fellowships at Dallas and at Sunshine-St Albans, they served in Zambia with the Australian Baptist Missionary Society, but after only twelve months ill-health forced their return home.

Hans recovered at Sale, Gippsland where he was involved in Church planting at Lakes Entrance. He later pastored at Aberfeldie in Melbourne and at Arncliffe in inner Sydney before accepting the Lenah Valley appointment.

Rev Malcolm Eberhard

Malcolm Eberhard was born at Blyth, SA, and grew up at Yacka and Crystal Brook in the mid-north of the State. In Adelaide he worked as a Civil Draftsman in the State and Commonwealth Governments and also as a draftsman in Bougainville (Papua, New Guinea). He was converted at a Crusade in Port Pirie in 1961. He trained at Burleigh Theological College, completing the Diploma of Theology. He had also completed a B.A. and an Honours degree in Philosophy. His M.A. degree in Evangelism and Communications was gained from Pacific College of Graduate Studies. His wife Doreen was a former teacher and they have three children. Prior to his time at Gumeracha in 1976-85, he had ministered at South Plympton, Hawthorndene and North Croydon Baptist Churches, all in SA and as an associate at the Glasshouse Country (Beerwah) Baptist Church in Queensland and finally back in SA at the Hackham Baptist Church for 2008 to 2016. Following his time at Lenah Valley which commenced in 1986, the family transferred to Maleny District Baptist Church in Queensland and at Mareeba.

Rev Paul Kerrison

Paul Kerrison was the third son of godly Methodist parents. In later years he attended the Margaret Street Church of Christ in Launceston being involved with youth groups and Christian Endeavour. At the completion of his apprenticeship, he commenced as a building contractor and later as a real estate salesman. He continued his church involvement with the Hobart Church of Christ. He trained in Sydney at the Churches of Christ Theological College (Carlingford N.S.W.) graduating with a

Diploma of Ministry and a Bachelor of Theology. He later undertook a Post Graduate-Diploma of Ministry in Pastoral Care.

He had ministries at Narraweena Church of Christ, at the Churches of Christ Theological College at Carlingford as part-time lecturer, the Portland Church of Christ and a one year interim ministry at the Howrah Church of Christ. His association with the Church of Christ continued until the Lenah Valley appointment.

Rev John Smith

John Smith was born in Booleroo Centre, South Australia, and grew up on the family farm. He became a fifth-generation farmer. The family attended the local Anglican Church, but following the touch of God on his life, he and his wife Heather began attending the Morphett Vale Baptist Church in Adelaide. Heather was a trained State Education teacher. The call to full-time ministry at Morphett Vale came and he became its Associate Pastor. For two years he attended the Bible College of S.A. and its joint venture, the New Creation Teaching Ministry. He then attended the Burleigh College from 1979 gaining a Diploma in Ministry. From 1982, at the completion of his studies at Burleigh, he was appointed Senior Pastor at Mount Barker Baptist Church. In 1992 he became Senior Pastor of the Mount Gambier Baptist also in SA.

Rev Matt Garvin

Matt Garvin was a former radio announcer and journalist who worked with Fusion Australia from 1992 to 2012 in Tasmania and Victoria, including two years in the international leadership of the mission movement. Matt and his wife Leeanne and family spent five years in Canada where Matt served as the Mission and Community Engagement Pastor at the St Albert Alliance Church, Alberta. While in Canada he gained a Master of Theological Studies at Taylor Seminary. Earlier he had gained a Graduate Certificate in Management at UTAS and an Advanced Diploma in

Youth and Community Work through Fusion Australia. Matt started at Citywide in July 2017.

Executive Pastor Dan Evenhuis

Dan Evenhuis recently lived and worked in the UK for eighteen years. He grew up in Smithton, Tasmania, and trained as a Mathematics and Science teacher. He with his wife Dani moved to the UK in 2004 to establish a Fusion youth and community network.

Dan's roles included being National Director, for seven years, head of administration, finances and office management, in charge of information technology which included Fusion's website, constituent database and network administration. Further he gave leadership to the youth work, church liaison and worked as youth and community work trainer.

In 2014, after ten years of ministry in the Wheatley area in Oxfordshire, which involved children's work, youth work and community events, and in agreement with the local churches, a new church was planted which would take the form of a less traditional evangelical church. The first service saw sixty-two attendees and it was a joy to Dan to see God build this church. This church, the Wheatley Community Church, is now an established local church with one full-time and three part-time employees.

LENAH VALLEY BAPTIST CHURCH TIMELINE

1 Aug 1948	A Sunday School was started by the Hobart Baptist Church (Rev E Roberts-Thomson) in the Community Hall, Creek Rd
7 Feb 1952	Morning services commenced in the RSL Hall at Lenah Valley followed by evening services on 24 Feb 1952
May – Oct 1953	**Rev John Toroni**
4 Nov 1953	Formal recognition of the Lenah Valley Baptist Fellowship
Apr 1954 – Mar 1957	**Rev Trevor Fist**
27 Nov 1954	A house was purchased ($5,000) for the church manse at 159 Augusta Rd
13 Jun 1956	Block of land purchased for $1,900 at 2 Pottery Rd, Lenah Valley
25 Nov 1956	First baptismal held at Hobart Baptist Church - Wanda King (nee Tapp) & Graeme Kelly were baptised
May 1958 – Mar 1961	**Rev Tom Green**
17 Jul 1960	Foundation stone was laid for the church building at 2 Pottery Rd
26 Nov 1960	Official opening of the church building built at a cost of $9,500
26 Feb 1961	Constitution of the church with a foundation membership of 21 people
7 May – Nov 1961	**Rev Martin Kerly - Interim ministry**

15 Aug 1961	Election of the first diaconate – Jessie Seville, Enid Kelly, Frank Kelly, Andrew Lawry, Cliff Jacks and Maurice French
20 Feb 1962	New Manse purchased at 22 Suncrest Ave for $13,200.
May - Nov 1962	**Pastor Allan Lehmann**
Jan – Feb 1962	**Pastor David Nibbs**
Nov 1962 – Mar 1963	**Pastor David Nibbs**
30 May 1963 – Jul 1966	**Rev Matthew Francis**
5 Feb 1967 – May 1971	**Rev Don Johnson**
Feb 1973 – Feb 1976	**Rev Don Cameron**
28 May 1977	Opening of the new hall extension built by subcontract for $20,000
June 1978 – Dec 1979	**Pastor Jim Yeo**
14 Feb 1981 – 2 Dec 1984	**Rev Hans Bohm**
14 Mar 1982 – Nov 1983	**Pastor Les Maus (Associate)**
5 Jul 1981	Worship services transferred to the new church hall due to increased attendances
Late 1983	Church services were moved to the Community Hall while the auditorium was enlarged
28 Jul 1984	Membership of the church now 80 with an average attendance at worship services of 130
28 Jul 1984	Opening of the new enlarged worship centre built by church people at a cost of $40,000
2 Feb 1986 – Dec 1990	**Rev Malcolm Eberhard**

16 Feb 1991 – Dec 1992 Pastor Peter Matthewson

19 Apr 1993 – Dec 1997 Rev Gary Piper

12 Feb 1999 – 3 Jul 2012 Rev Paul Kerrison

May 2005	Office & Front Entry added to church building
6 Apr 2008	Lenah Valley Church joined with Citygate Church to become Citywide Baptist Church

Feb 2009 – Mar 2015   Rev Maddy Svoboda (Youth Pastor & later Pastor responsible for Lenah Valley)

Jun 2011	Hobart Nepalese Church commenced to meet with the Lenah Valley congregation

May 2015 – Jan 2017   Rev David Roffe (Interim Pastor)

1 Jul 2015 – Dec 2021   Pastor Dan Hutchison (Youth Pastor & Associate Pastor from 1 Jul 2017)

Jul 2017 - Present   Rev Matt Garvin

25 Feb 2018	Hobart Nepalese Church formally joined as another congregation of Citywide Baptist Church

25 Feb 2018 - Present   Nepalese Pastor Paul Rai

5 Aug 2018	Special Service & followed by lunch at the RSL club to celebrate the 70th anniversary of the commencement of the church in Lenah Valley

30 Jan 2022 - Present   Dan Evenhuis Executive Pastor

6 Aug 2023	Special Service & lunch with an afternoon to celebrate the 75th anniversary of the church in Lenah Valley with the launch of the book "75 Years of Christian Witness"

www.ingramcontent.com/pod-product-compliance
Lightning Source LLC
Chambersburg PA
CBHW062113290426
44110CB00023B/2801